CHESS

BY
Paul Langfield

ILLUSTRATED BY
Ed Carr

MACDONALD

First published 1979

Macdonald Educational Ltd
Holywell House
Worship Street
London EC2A 2EN

© Macdonald Educational 1979
ISBN 0 356 06329 1 (paperback)
ISBN 0 356 06369 0 (hardback)

Printed by New Interlitho,
Milan, Italy

About this book

This book has been carefully planned to help you become an expert. Look for the special pages to find the information you need. **RECOGNITION** pages, with a **brown flash** in the top right-hand corner, contain all the essential information to know and remember. **PROJECT** pages, with a **grey border,** suggest some interesting ideas for things to do and make. At the end of the book there is a useful **REFERENCE** section.

The aim of the game

▲The board laid out
ready for a game of
chess.

Hunt the King!

Chess is a battle between the White and Black
pieces. Attacks are launched by each player and
pieces are taken, with the aim of weakening your
opponent's forces and eventually checkmating your
opponent's King – that is, trapping him without
escape. Of course, he'll be trying to checkmate you,
too.

When one of your pieces can capture the enemy
King in his next move, the King is in check. If the
King can escape, the game continues. If not, you
have won. Now place the pieces on the board as
shown above to learn how they move.

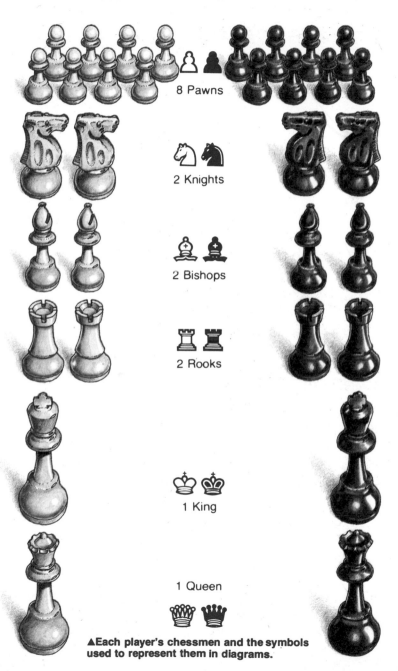

8 Pawns

2 Knights

2 Bishops

2 Rooks

1 King

1 Queen

▲Each player's chessmen and the symbols used to represent them in diagrams.

Understanding the board

The field of battle
The board for chess is the same as that for draughts (checkers). Both the black and white squares are used. Pieces move in many different ways. The three main directions are along **Ranks, Files** and **Diagonals.**

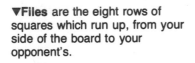

◀The Ranks
The rows of squares which run across the board from left to right are the Ranks. If you were playing White you would be seated at the foot of the board. Note that each player has a **white square** in the right-hand corner.

At the start of a game, each player's pieces stand on his first two Ranks. Several pieces are allowed to move along the Ranks.

▼Diagonals are the rows of squares between you and your opponent, if moves are made across the corners of the squares.

▼Files are the eight rows of squares which run up, from your side of the board to your opponent's.

▲Rows of Diagonals.

◀Diagonals only cover squares of the same colour, while Ranks and Files have both black and white squares.

▼The board has a **King's side** and a **Queen's side.** For White the King's side is on the right and the Queen's side on the left. For Black it's the other way round.

So if White moves strongly on the right-hand side of the board, we call it a King's side attack.

▼The central squares.

▲In the opening aim to control the **central squares,** marked above.

QUEEN'S SIDE

KING'S SIDE

BLACK

WHITE

▶Here is a chess diagram of the pieces ready for a game. White is always shown playing from the bottom of the picture and Black from the top. Note that the Queens are always placed on squares of their own colour.

7

How the ROOKS move

The long move
Rooks (also sometimes known as castles) can move as far as you want, but only on Ranks and Files. Each player starts with two Rooks on the corner squares. They can't move yet, because they can only move along empty squares. The Rook is a powerful piece and can advance or retreat.

▼The Rooks in this diagram can be moved to any of the squares marked with a cross. Their long range makes them very valuable pieces.

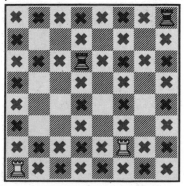

How to capture
The Rooks on the left cannot, in the next move, capture each other. If, however, opposing Rooks stood in the same Rank or File, they could take each other.

In chess, a piece is **taken** when another piece moves onto its square. The captured piece is then out of the game. You can't take your own pieces.

Take care not to let your Rooks be taken. Always try to move them to safe squares.

▲The white King is **checked** by the black Rook. Look below to find out how White can save himself.

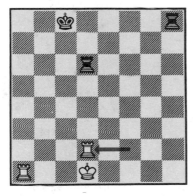

▲Rook as defender
Here we see White has moved his Rook to the square immediately above that of the King. Now the King is no longer in check, and the white Rook is threatening the black one.

Now Black must decide whether to take the white Rook, or to defend his own Rook by moving his other Rook alongside his King.

▼In this position, the white Rook can capture the black Bishop.

If it's Black's turn to move, his Rook can take the white Pawn. White Rook can put black King in check. Black needs two moves to put white King in check.

▼If it is White's turn to move, his Rook can capture the black Pawn. It cannot capture the Bishop (why not?).

Black has a choice if it's his turn to move. He can protect the Pawn by moving his Rook into the same Rank or File as the Pawn. Or his Rook could check White's King.

How the BISHOPS move

Ruling the Diagonals

Each player has one Bishop using white squares and one using black squares, and they remain on the same colour squares throughout the game. They can only move diagonally, across the corners of the squares. Bishops can also both advance and retreat.

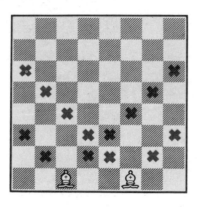

◄The Bishop's Diagonals
These two white Bishops are in their starting positions. They can move to any of the squares indicated, because those squares are unoccupied. If a black piece were on one of those squares, the white Bishop could take it.

At the beginning of a game Bishops are like Rooks – they cannot be moved until there are empty squares in front of them.

►Capturing with a Bishop
These black Bishops are threatening three white pieces. Can you see how?

The Bishop next to the King, known as the King's Bishop, could capture White's Rook or his Knight.

And the Queen's Bishop (next to the Queen) is in a position to take the white pawn.

▼Check!
The black Bishop has put the white King in check, as shown. White must now move his King out of the way.

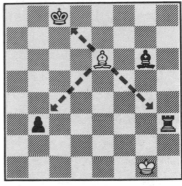

▲A strong Bishop
The white Bishop checks the black King, which must move. White can then use his Bishop to take either the black Pawn or the Rook.

▶Strength in the centre
The white Bishops are better placed than the black ones, because they are on centre squares. They each control 13 squares, while the Bishops at the side of the board can only capture on 7 squares.

But here Black has the white King in check, so White must first move his King.

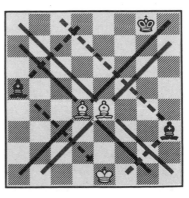

How the PAWNS move

The foot soldiers

If you think of chess as a battle, Pawns are the foot soldiers. It is usual to start the game with a Pawn, which can advance one or two squares. Then they go forward one square at a time. Pawns cannot go backwards. And if they reach the end of their File they are promoted into another piece of the player's choice.

◄A Pawn opening
Here's how the Pawns often start a game of chess. White moves his King Pawn (the Pawn in front of his King) two squares forward. Black makes the same move.

White cannot capture the black Pawn, because **Pawns capture diagonally,** though they move up the File.

So in this position, the Pawns are blocking each other and can't move.

▼A Pawn capture
These Pawns can take each other because they are in adjacent diagonal squares.

▼Promoting a Pawn
If a Pawn survives until the end of a game, it can become very important. That's because, if the Pawn reaches the end of the Board, it can become any piece the player wishes (except a King). Here the Pawn, because it takes diagonally, has Black's King in check. Read on to see what happens (below left).

▼Pawn becomes Queen
Black decided to move his King out of the way. But as a result White's Pawn moved on to the last Rank. White then had the choice of what piece the Pawn would become. And here it is, as an all-powerful Queen!
 White should now win.

Summary
Pawn moves are more varied than those of the other pieces.
 Pawns move forward, one square at a time, except for their first move when they can advance two squares.
 Pawns capture with a diagonal move. Pawns can also be promoted.

How the QUEENS move

The mighty monarch

Queens are the most powerful of all the chess pieces. This is because they have greater mobility than any of the others. The Queen can move like a Rook or a Bishop: that is, along either Ranks, Files or Diagonals.

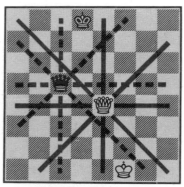

◀The Queen's power

Both Queens stand on central squares of the board. The solid lines show the moves which the white Queen could make. The broken lines cover the squares ruled by the black Queen.

In this position neither of the Kings is in check from a Queen. But each Queen can check on their next move.

The Exchange

Your Queen is valuable and should be guarded carefully throughout the game.

But there are times when it's worth swopping pieces. That is, you allow your Queen to be taken, provided you can take your opponent's Queen.

If you make an exchange, make sure you have enough strength with your other pieces to checkmate.

▼In this game, it's White's turn to move. He decides to use his Queen to take the black Queen, knowing she will be taken by the black King. But White has already planned his next move, as you will see below.

▼White having taken the black Queen, black King captures the white Queen. He has no other choice.

The white Rook in the corner sweeps down the Rank, and as a result . . .

▲Checkmate!

▼A hard choice
Here the black Queen has the white King in check. The King must move out of check, and then the black Queen will be able to capture either the white Pawn or Bishop.

Although Bishops are usually stronger than Pawns, here Black must take the white Pawn. Otherwise it will promote into a Queen and check Black's King.

How the KNIGHTS move

The L-shaped jump

The way a Knight moves is best thought of as an L-shaped jump. It can go **either** two squares up or down and one square left or right; **or** two squares left or right and one square up or down. It is the only chess piece which is allowed to jump over other pieces – your own or your opponent's.

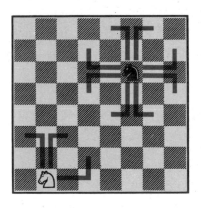

◄The white Knight is in its starting position, and can go to only 3 squares. Black's Knight has made its first move, and now has the choice of 8 squares. If another piece were on any of those 8 squares the Knight could take it.

We can see that by aiming for the important central squares of the board, the black Knight has gained a stronger position.

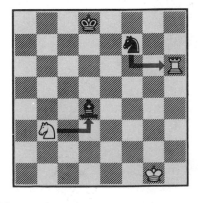

►Here the white Knight can capture the black Bishop. And the black Knight is ready to capture the white Rook.

A Knight can check the opponent's King if it lands on a square from which it threatens to take the King.

Each Knight shown here would have to make two moves to put the enemy King in check.

▲The start of a game, where two Pawns and two Knights have moved.

▼Black's Knight is now able to take the white Knight. Knights are worth more than Pawns, as you can see from the chart on pages 26-27, so Black has come off best in this exchange.

▲The white Knight takes the black Pawn. Read on to find out why this was a bad move.

The Knight's value
The Knight is a very useful piece. Although it can't cross long distances, it can leap to and fro around every square of the board.

Also, it can jump over your own or your opponent's pieces in an unexpected way.

How the KINGS move

Your opponent's target
The game of chess is basically a combination of attacking your opponent's King and defending your own. The King's movement is limited, to only one square in any direction, except for a special move called castling (see pages 22-23).

▼Check
The white King is in check from the black Rook. At all times try to keep your King on a square where it cannot be checked.

▲Moving to safety
The King moves to the next File and gets out of check.

Moving the King out of check to a safe square is not the only way to escape. If you still have other pieces on the board, they may be able to block the check, or capture the attacking piece.

▲Blocking check
In this illustration the black King is in check from the white Bishop.

Black's best move would be to move his Bishop into the diagonal between his King and the white Bishop. Then Black's Bishop would protect his King, and threaten to take the white Bishop.

After that, White might choose to exchange Bishops. Or he might move his Bishop to avoid its capture.

▼Taking the attacker
The white King is in check from the black Knight. White can take the attacking Knight, however.

Kings on the attack
Kings can capture enemy pieces, but only if they are unprotected. Otherwise the King would be moving into check.

▼The black King, in the middle of the board, has much greater mobility than the white King in the corner.

You should remember that this also makes the black King more vulnerable to attack, if there are other pieces on the board.

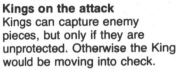

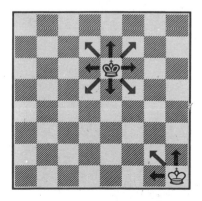

▲Kings cannot stand next to each other – they would be moving into check. White King here is all right in all the squares shown but would not be in those with crosses.

Chart of the moves

Here is a summary of how the different pieces move and the rules which govern their movements.

It is usual to open a game with a Pawn because until these have moved – usually the centre pawns – no other pieces except the Knights can move.

What is important is to use your pieces together, so that you can capture enemy pieces and so weaken his forces. But, except when you castle, you can move only one piece when it is your turn.

Pawns

Pawns move forward along the Files. They never retreat. Their first move can cover one or two squares, then it's one square at a time.

They capture pieces diagonally – here White has a choice of black Pawns to take. The white Pawn on the right can advance to be promoted into a Queen.

Rooks

Rooks can move as far along any Rank or File on which they stand as the player wishes. If an enemy piece occupies the Rank or File, the Rook can take it.

Here the white Rooks can capture Bishop or Knight. One black Rook can take a white Pawn, the other checks the white King.

Knights

Knights jump two squares up and one across, or one square up and two across.

On the right, one white Knight can capture Black's Rook, the other has the black King in check.

But a black Knight can capture the checking Knight. And both black Knights can take White's pawn.

Bishops

Bishops travel only along Diagonals.

In this position both white Bishops can take a black Rook.

One black Bishop can capture White's Knight. The other checks the white King, and can capture the white Pawn which is about to promote.

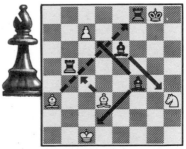

Queens

The powerful Queens can use Ranks, Files or Diagonals.

This game shows Black's Queen checking White, and threatening his Rook.

The white Queen threatens Black's Rook and Pawn. But White must first get out of check.

Kings

A King can move only one square, in any direction, except when castling (pages 22-23).

This black King can take White's Bishop, and the white King can take the black Pawn.

At the end of the game Kings often join in the attack, but at all times they must be carefully guarded.

How to castle

Castling – a special move

Each player may castle once in any game. The King and one Rook are moved together if they have not already moved and if the squares between them are vacant. The King must not cross a square under attack.

▲White about to castle on the King's side.

The aim of castling

The aim of castling is to put the King on a safer side square, and to bring the Rook to the centre where it can attack.

You can castle only once in a game, on either the King's side or Queen's side.

In each case, providing there is no piece between King and Rook, the King moves two squares along the Rank towards the Rook, which hops to the other side of the King.

▼White has castled on the King's side.

▲White has castled on the Queen's side.

▲Black has castled on the King's side.

▲Black has castled on the Queen's side.

The en passant *move*

Caught in passing

This is a special kind of Pawn capture, which it's easy to forget – until your Pawn is taken!

It takes place when a Pawn of either side has reached the fifth Rank, and an enemy Pawn in either adjacent File has not yet moved.

In this position, shown below, if the white Pawn advances two squares, trying to get by in passing (French: *en passant*), it can be taken as though it had advanced only one square.

So whether the white Pawn moves one or two squares forward it can be taken.

If the player intends to make an *en passant* capture, his move must follow immediately that of the advancing Pawn.

▼Black's Pawn is on his fifth Rank.

▲Whether the white Pawn advances two squares,

▼or just one – it is taken.

▶**Taken *en passant***
Here's the position after the *en passant* capture. After either of the positions shown above, black Pawn takes white Pawn, moving to the square shown on the right.

It's not often that this possibility comes about. But if you miss the position you may be very sorry.

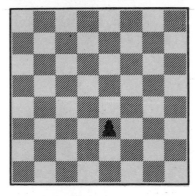

What each piece is worth

Not all chess pieces have the same value. The chart on the right shows that a Bishop or Knight is worth 3 Pawns, a Rook is more valuable, and the Queen can be worth more than all your Pawns. The King, of course, is priceless – lose your King and you lose the game.

▼The white Queen is about to checkmate by taking the Pawn next to the black King. What can Black do?

Black can defend the attacked Pawn with a Knight or Rook, so that if the white Queen takes the Pawn, the Queen in turn is taken.

Black may otherwise decide attack is the best form of defence – if black Knight takes white Knight, it is White who is in check.

▼Here Black's Bishop can take the white Rook. But this would be a mistake, because then the white Knight would capture the black Queen, putting Black in check.

Whenever you intend to capture an opponent's piece, first make sure that you don't have any piece of higher value which can be taken.

Here Black should first move his Queen to a safe square. Then Black should win.

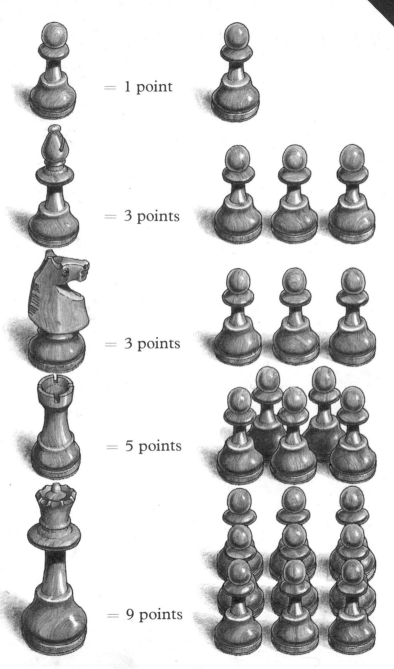

= 1 point

= 3 points

= 3 points

= 5 points

= 9 points

Draws and stalemates

Sometimes neither player is able to force a win, and as a result the game is drawn. If neither side has enough pieces to force mate, it's also drawn. But even a player with stronger pieces can make a mistake, and let his weaker opponent lead him into a drawn position.

◄Too few pieces
White has only a Knight left, and Black is reduced to a single Bishop. Neither player has enough material to force mate, so the players should agree on a draw.

In a position like this, if either player had a single Pawn, he would have a good chance of winning by advancing the Pawn to promote.

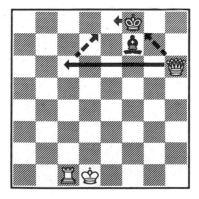

◄Perpetual check
Black King moves as shown to escape check. White Queen checks as shown by the solid arrow. If the King returns to his original square, and White keeps checking from the same squares, Black has a draw by repetition of moves.

If you are losing, but can keep the opponent in perpetual check, it's a lucky escape. But here White throws away a win.

▶Stalemate

White cannot win, and Black has enough pieces to mate quickly. But then Black moves his King as shown.

The result is stalemate – there is no move that White can make without putting himself in check, which is obviously not allowed. So White has a lucky draw.

▶Another lucky draw

White should checkmate on this move. But instead of moving his Queen or Rook to Black's back Rank and winning, he moves his Knight as indicated.

Black isn't in check. His Pawn is blocked and so can't move. And if his King moves it will place itself in check.

Stalemate again, and Black has a draw.

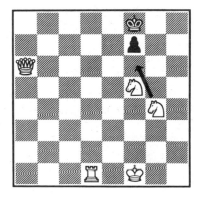

▶The careless Queen

However powerful your pieces are in an ending, and however weak the opposition's, you should always be alert.

Here White's Queen closes in for the kill, as the arrow shows. But there is no move left for Black – and he's not in check.

As here, stalemate often results from a mistake.

Chess notation

Descriptive Notation is common in the UK and USA, while **Algebraic** Notation is common on the Continent and in the USSR. Either enables you to record your own games or follow other's games.

Individual pieces are identified by the side of the board they stand on. So from left to right, you start with Queen's Rook, Queen's Knight etc. Pawns and Files are named in turn after these pieces: Queen's Rook Pawn, and so on.

Some symbols
P=Pawn   ch or + = check
R=Rook   0−0 = castles on King's side
N=Knight   0−0−0 = castles on Queen's side
B=Bishop   e.p. = *en passant*
Q=Queen   ! = good move
K=King   ? = bad move

Descriptive Notation
Each player writes his move, with the File as seen from his end and numbered 1-8. So the King's Pawn advancing two squares is written, P-K4.

Algebraic Notation
The Algebraic System uses a map reference system. The Ranks are numbered 1-8, always from White's end. The Files become the letters a-h. When a piece moves, you write its initial and the square it moves to. With Pawns just give the square moved to. So the King's Pawn move P-K4 is simply e4.

▲ Descriptive Notation

▼ Algebraic Notation

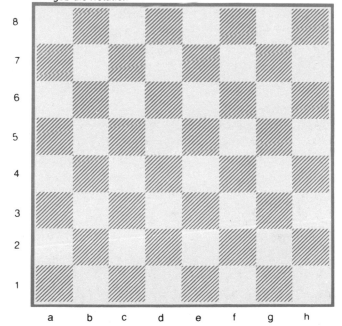

8 7 6 5 4 3 2 1

a b c d e f g h

Opening a game

What to move?
The first move is always made by White. Advancing
one of the centre Pawns is a good idea – it takes
control of the important central squares, and allows
other pieces like the Bishop room to move. Don't
hurry to attack – develop your pieces first.

▶White and Black both opened
with P-K4. White then played
N-KB3 to attack the black Pawn.
Black played N-QB3 which
protects his Pawn. That is if
White plays NxP then Black
replies NxN! Now White attacks
black Knight by bringing out his
King Bishop. Black moves his
Queen Rook Pawn one square
which threatens the Bishop.

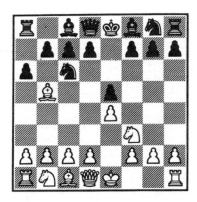

▶Here White opened with his
Queen Pawn and Black blocked
it with his. Each player
developed his Queen's Knight.
White brought out his other
Knight and Black attacked it with
his Bishop. White then tried to
drive the Bishop away with his
Rook Pawn. Black Bishop can
go B-KR4 or play BxN.

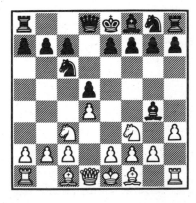

◄This opening is called the **Sicilian Defence.** White plays P-K4 and Black replies with P-QB4, neither blocking nor attacking White's Pawn. The next move for White is N-KB3 and Black plays N-QB3. Then comes the challenge. White plays P-Q4. The black Pawn can now capture it. But then White can take Black's Pawn with his Knight which makes the captures equal.

◄Here White starts with P-Q4 and Black plays N-KB3. White brings out his Queen Bishop Pawn to occupy one of the outer centre squares. Black answers with P-QB4. White can of course capture this Pawn. An alternative move for White which may be to his advantage later is P-Q5. Note that if Black then plays NxP, White replies with PxN.

◄This is called the **English Opening.** White starts with P-QB4 and Black goes P-K4. White then plays N-QB3 and Black N-KB3. Both players then bring out their other Knights. White can capture Black's Pawn but would be foolish to do so because it would be followed by NxN. For the next few moves both players should mobilize more pieces.

Middle game play

Beware of traps!
Things can get very complicated in the middle game, with several pieces involved. **Pins, Forks** and **Skewers** are among the traps you can easily fall into. In each of the examples below, you'll find more in the position than first meets the eye.

▶The Pin

A piece is pinned if it cannot, or should not move – because, by doing so, it opens another piece to attack.

In this example the white Knight is pinned. White cannot move it, because to do so would put his own King in check from Black's Queen.

▶The trapped Rook

Here the black Rook is pinned. Black may move if he wishes but he will lose his Queen to White's Bishop if he does so. Black can, of course, save his Queen by moving her, or interposing his Knight.

▶A deadly Fork

A fork is an attack on more than one piece in a single move.

On the right, White's King's Knight, on the sixth Rank, threatens the black King and Queen. The King must move out of check, and on the next move the Knight takes the Queen.

▶The Skewer

A skewer is a disguised attack, when the real target lies beyond the enemy piece threatened.

Here the white Bishop has Black's King in check. But the real reason the Bishop was placed there is that, when the King moves out of check, the Rook can be taken.

▶Skewering a Fork

It looks as though White has a powerful fork, with his Knight attacking Black's King and Rook.

But Black can unleash a skewer, by taking the Knight with his Bishop. Then White must move his King and lose his Rook.

The end game

How to checkmate

It is important to checkmate with the fewest possible moves. The end usually comes when both players have captured pieces, and there are few chessmen left on the board. That's when you've got to seize your opportunity to win.

The cornered King

At the end of a game, the King is often in at the kill of the enemy King.

Here, for example, Black's King has crowded the white King in the corner, cutting off his escape when the Queen comes in to check.

It's easier to mate a King which is caught in the corner.

Mated in a net

Two pieces combine here to checkmate Black's King.

While it's the Bishop that has the King in check, the Queen is the piece that cuts off all four possible escape squares.

Here the King is caught in a net thrown out by two pieces.

Kings need guarding

Though White still has a Knight and Bishop, both are in the wrong position to protect the white King.

The black Queen moves in to the square in front of the King for a simple checkmate.

White has left all the squares round his King unprotected.

Smothered mate

This checkmate often occurs when a King has castled. The King, tucked in the corner, is suddenly smothered by its own Pawns, when the White Rook checks.

So Black contributes to his own defeat, by not having moved one of his three Pawns forward to allow escape.

Combined attack

Use as many pieces as you can in your attack. In this position, it takes Bishop, Knight and Rook to make sure the white King has no safe square to move to.

It's easy to put a King in check. It's much harder to make sure he can't get out of check.

A chess game

Here is a short game to play on your own board. The opening is called the **Danish Gambit**. White wins by making early sacrifices to ensure that he gets better development in the opening moves. Black defends well and manages a fairly good attack but, despite his threat to White from his Queen and Knight, Black cannot checkmate because he is constantly forced to make defensive moves.

	WHITE	**BLACK**
1.	P – K4	P – K4
2.	P – Q4	P x P
3.	P – QB3	P x P
4.	B – QB4	N – KB3

It looks as though Black is in the lead. He has captured two Pawns but White expected this and, though he has taken chances, he still expects to win because his pieces are better developed.

5.	N – B3	B – B4
6.	N x P	P – Q3

(See **Fig. 1**).

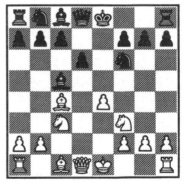

Fig. 1

White stops further Pawn captures and Black protects his Bishop with a Pawn.

7.	O – O	O – O
8.	N – KN5	P – KR3

Both players castle and White advances a Knight into enemy territory while Black tries to drive it away with a Pawn.

9.	N x P	R x N

A daring sacrifice by White. If you look at the points value of the captures he is now 3 points down.

38

10. P – K5   N – N5

Black cannot play P x P without
losing his Queen! He saves his
Knight by moving it.

11. P – K6   Q – R5
12. P x R ch   K – B1

Black King could not capture the
Pawn because White Bishop is
on the same diagonal (**Fig. 2.**)

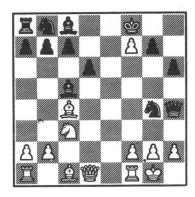

Fig. 2

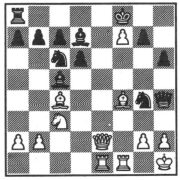

Fig. 3

13. B – B4   N x BP
14. Q – K2   N – N5

This is a discovered check from
Black's Bishop.

15. K – R1   B – Q2
16. QR – K1   N – QB3

White now has a strong King
side attack. Black's last move
clears the way for his Rook to
come into play. (**Fig. 3**)

17. Q – K8 ch   R x Q
18. P x R (Q) ch   B x Q

White could afford to sacrifice
his Queen *and* his Queened
Pawn. Black's moves were
forced. He had no alternatives.

19. B x QP Mate! (**Fig. 4**)

Black King is in check from both
Bishop and Rook. There is no
flight square. Black had hoped
to play Q x RP mate but White
was too strong for him. A very

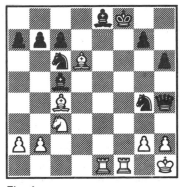

Fig. 4

sharp little game.

Computers play chess

▲ Playing a game of chess with Boris the computer.

▶Two other types of chess computer at present available.

Man against machine

There are literally millions of possible moves in a game of chess. But in this age of computers, machines have now been developed which can give all but the very best players a good game.

Chess computers are still expensive, costing about £100. Machines like the 'Chess Challenger 10' can be adjusted to different levels of play, from beginner to expert. The Challenger is familiar with over 3 million board positions, and knows all the special moves – promotion of pawns, *en passant* and castling.

An expert opponent

Another advanced computer is called 'Boris'. When you play Boris, you not only have a hard game, but you are treated to comments from the computer, like 'I expected that', or 'Illegal move' if you try to cheat!

Both these micro-computers are beautifully made, in luxury cases and complete with board and pieces. It's likely that cheaper chess machines will soon be made – but for the time being humans still make the best opponents!

The Turk
A Hungarian engineer, Baron Wolfgang von Kempelen, invented the first automatic chess player in the 18th century. It made its appearance in 1770 at the court of the Empress Maria Theresa. In fact, of course, it was a hoax, but one that baffled experts for many years. Even now no one is absolutely sure how it was worked but it is known that a concealed human player operated it from inside the cabinet. The Turk almost always beat its opponent. A human computer, in fact!

Other forms of chess

History of chess

The game of chess has evolved from an Indian war
game which was first played some time in the fifth
or sixth century A.D. As the game moved to western
countries it became the chess we play today.

Eastern countries have evolved rather different
forms of the game. Books of instructions and
complete sets are available for those interested.

Chinese chess (Hsiang Ch'i)

The pieces are round discs with Chinese characters
engraved on them. European players find them hard
to tell apart so it is a good idea to paste Western
symbols on to them. The King in this game is an
Emperor. Both players also have two each of the
following: Mandarins, Elephants, Knights, Rooks,
Cannons, and five Pawns.

The **board** is usually printed on paper. The
horizontal division in the centre is supposed to be
the Great Yellow River of China.

 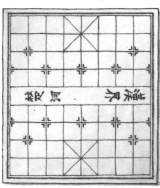

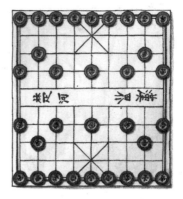

►Playing Chinese chess
Play takes place on the
intersection of the lines and not on
the squares. The small squares
marked with diagonal lines are the
fortresses beyond which neither
Emperor nor Mandarins can
move. On the right you can see
the printed board with pieces set
up ready for a game. The object of
the game is to checkmate the
enemy Emperor.

Japanese chess (Shogi)

This version of chess probably had its beginnings in
the eighth century A.D., a little later than Chinese
and Indian chess.

Shogi pieces are of the same colour for both
players and are distinguished from each other by the
direction in which they are pointed. The pieces have
romantic names: Silver General, Gold General, Spear
etc.

The pieces have black markings on one side and,
when promoted, are turned over to reveal red
markings. If you want to learn, Shogi books and sets
are available.

Japanese chess
Pieces point in the direction they
move. They are marked in black
on one side and red on the other.

43

Chess variants

A number of variations on the standard game of chess have been invented, and have had some popularity. Here are brief outlines of a few.

Losing game
The rules are quite different in this game. You expose your pieces to capture, and capturing is compulsory. The aim is to lose all your pieces or be stalemated. Check and checkmate do not apply. Pawns can be promoted, but in this game, to King only.

Scotch chess
White opens with one move and Black replies with two moves. White may then make three followed by Black making four moves and so on. You may only check your opponent in the last move of any sequence. If your opponent cannot get out of check in his first next move, he is mated.

Three-dimensional chess

In this game the rules of conventional chess are applied to one set of chessmen played on three boards. White moves first but Black is entitled to decide on which plane he will play. One player must start on the top plane and the other on the bottom plane. Any piece being moved for the first time must change one plane.

▲Three-dimensional chess being played on transparent boards, mounted one above the other.

Hexagonal Chess

Most of the rules of conventional chess apply, but not only is the board different in shape, the squares are also hexagonal and pieces have more freedom of movement.

In addition to this each player starts the game with three Bishops instead of the two, and nine instead of eight Pawns. Sets with hexagonal board, extra pieces and rules of the game are available.

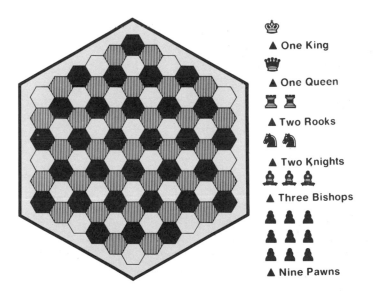

▲ One King

▲ One Queen

▲ Two Rooks

▲ Two Knights

▲ Three Bishops

▲ Nine Pawns

Chess pieces of the world

◀**Reynard the Fox.** Based on the characters in a story by two Flemish poets of the 13th century. A German writer, Goethe, published a translation in 1857 and an artist called von Kaulbac illustrated the book. He also made the chess pieces which are now in a Munich museum.

◀**Carved African set.** These pieces come from Kenya. The King is a tribal chief. The Rooks are tall mud huts and the Knights long-necked giraffes. Pawns are the heads of native warriors, all beautifully carved.

◀**The Lewis sets.** A well-known set carved in the 11th or 12th century, and found in an underground chamber on the Isle of Lewis, off the coast of Scotland, in 1831. Carved from walrus tusk (morse ivory), these sets are now in the British Museum, London, and the National Museum, Edinburgh.

◀**The Eight Immortals.** A chess set based on classical Chinese legends. These mythical figures include one woman and she is the Queen in the set. Stories of the Eight Immortals have been popular for many centuries in China.

◄Chinese carved ivory. Made in the early 19th century these pieces are carved from Indian ivory and then stained. The King is a mandarin and his wife is the Queen. Some of these sets were produced with pieces in natural ivory and ivory stained bright red.

◄Buddha chess set. Another early 19th century carved ivory set. This one comes from Ceylon. The 'black' pieces have been stained green, and the Pawns and Bishops resemble temple cupolas or decorations.

◄German medieval set. These pieces look a little like the Lewis sets but are of a slightly later period. The Kings have elaborately carved thrones surmounted by a lion. The back of the Queen's throne has carvings of ladies-in-waiting and musicians.

Staunton pieces
Designed in 1835 by Nathaniel Cook and named after the famous British player Howard Staunton, these sets have now become the universally accepted standard all over the world. The original sets have a small crown stamped on one Rook and one Knight, and are valuable.

A chess quiz

Problems to solve

Try setting up the pieces on your board as shown below. Turn the board, depending on whether you are asked to be Black or White, and see if you can find the right moves (these are given on page 58). The problems get progressively harder.

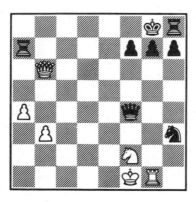

1. Can White win?

Black has a Rook and a Pawn more than White. And Black's Queen pins the white Knight.

It's White's turn to move. Despite the threats to his own King, White finds a way to win on the next move.

You are playing White. Can you see the move that gives you checkmate?

2. Instant victory

This time you are playing Black. You're in a slightly better position and there are several moves to choose from.

But there is one move you can make that brings checkmate on the move.

Look at what each piece could do, and try to find the instant checkmate.

3. Resisting temptation
Again you have the Black pieces.

Your Knight can take the white Queen. This would give you a material advantage, even after White's Bishop captures the black Rook.

But look again, and see if there isn't a much quicker way to win the game.

4. A mating combination
You are playing White. With the right move, you can launch an attack which leads to mate in three moves whatever Black does.

Black has the advantage of more pieces, and his Pawn forks the two white Knights.

Can you see how White can still win?

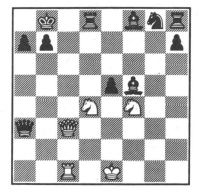

5. Now or never
Again Black has more pieces. As White, you have to find a way to attack the Black King, before Black launches his own attack.

What is White's correct move? And how many moves does he need to checkmate?

Answers: page 58

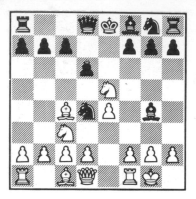

6. Don't take the Queen!
As indicated, White has moved his Knight to King 5. Now your black Bishop can take White's Queen.

But this is a trap. Why should you not take the Queen? And what is Black's correct move?

7. Checkmate in one
White can move and checkmate. The white Pawn can promote into a Queen, either by taking the Knight or moving forward a square.

Then the Pawn can become any piece – but does that bring checkmate?

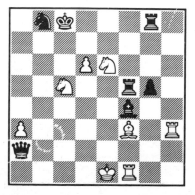

8. Which piece mates?
Another checkmate on the move for White. Black's pieces are worth 26 points, White's are worth only 21. But White can win now. How?

Answers: page 58

9. Fool's mate

We've already seen that it's best to advance centre and not side Pawns in the opening. Here White remembered and Black did not.

As White, checkmate next move.

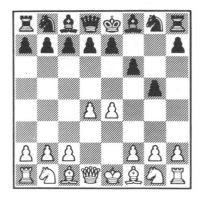

10. Easy!

Another side Pawn horror! Once more Black has moved his side Pawns, while White develops well in the centre.

You should not have too much trouble in seeing White's checkmate move.

11. Did you spot it?

Look at the front cover of this book. Can you spot the mistake?

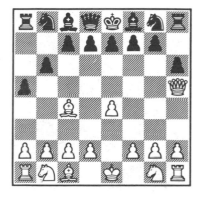

Chess clocks

In tournaments chess clocks are used to time each player. The player is told how many moves he must make within a given time. Forty moves an hour is usual.

When White has made a move he presses the button on his side of the clock and this starts Black's clock. After Black has moved he then presses his button and this starts White's clock.

Both players can see at a glance how much time they have left.

Making a chess set

▼Moulds
Chess pieces can be made quite easily from rubber moulds. These are available from toy or hobby shops but in case of difficulty write to the makers listed on page 62.

▼Fillings
You can use any moulding powder but the most satisfactory is Stonecast which dries harder than ordinary powder.

An alternative and even more durable material is resin, but this is rather messy and gives off pungent fumes which can be harmful.

Using resin
Make sure your room is well ventilated, and work near an open window.

Resin packs are available and these come complete with moulding powder and hardener. The resin is in a tin and looks like treacle. The powder should be added to the resin and when mixed you add the hardener. You need a container for mixing in; **paper cups** are ideal for small quantities.

A **box with holes** cut in it makes a suitable **support** for the moulds. The holes should be a little smaller than the edges of the moulds.

▼Cut holes in a cardboard box to support the moulds.

mixing Stonecast

▼Filling the mould
Half fill the mould, then pinch it to get rid of air bubbles. These make holes in the casting.

Now fill the rest of the mould. Continue to squeeze and then place in the support.

filling the mould

Much easier and safer to use is **Stonecast.** This is supplied in bags with a built-in hardener. You also need water. The proportions are three of Stonecast to one of water, measured by bulk. The powder should be sprinkled onto the water and slowly stirred. This avoids lumps. Allow the mixture to settle and avoid making bubbles.

Removing the mould
Stonecast dries quickly in a warm room. When hard, remove the casting by putting soap over the outside of the mould before peeling it off.

the finished pieces

Painting the pieces

▼A smooth finish
Before starting to colour pieces it is best to ensure a smooth base for them by rubbing each piece on a sheet of sandpaper.

sandpaper

Painting the pieces
Stonecast or moulding powder can be coloured with ordinary poster paints. You will also need some brushes, and old saucers for mixing the paints. Allow the colour to dry before adding a coat of **varnish**.

the paints you will need

▼The 'professional' touch
When the varnish has dried you can provide a nice finish to the pieces by adding felt to the bases.

felt

Coloured felt is sold in small squares by many general stores and hobby shops. You will need **glue** and a pair of sharp **scissors.**

Smear glue on the base of each piece, attach small squares of felt and then trim to shape *(see opposite)*.

▲Painting resin pieces
Resin pieces can be painted with oil colours and then varnished. Resin comes in natural (ivory) colour and black.

varnish

▼Metallic wax finishes
You can also finish off your chess pieces with metallic wax. This comes in gold, silver and bronze.

waxes

Using metallic waxes
If the pieces are made of Stonecast, it is a good idea to paint them first. Copper, gold or bronze are particularly effective when smeared on black pieces. These wax finishes are best applied with a finger. Alternatively you can use a small piece of clean rag.

▲Staining compound
Resin can be treated with a special staining compound which is painted on and then rubbed down with a cleaning fluid. The effect produced is that of an antique piece. This fluid should be kept in its glass bottle. Don't pour it into a plastic cup. It will melt the plastic!

▲The final touch: trimming the felt base.

Making a chess board

It is very satisfying to play chess on a board which you have made yourself. You can make boards out of coloured paper, squares of lino, or wood. Here is one way to make an attractive board.

You will need a solid base which is square. Chipboard is ideal.

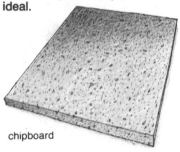

chipboard

The other requirements are sandpaper, a trimming knife, and dark and light wood veneers.

You will also need a steel rule or one with a metal edge, a set square, a pencil, sticky tape and a tube of glue.

▼Cutting the strips.

The size of your chessboard
The size of the squares you make for the board will be governed by the size of your chess pieces. If the King is an average size you will need squares 5 × 5cm. Your baseboard will need to be 40 × 40cm, or slightly bigger if you want a border.

▲Five strips of light and four of dark veneer. The strips should be 5cm wide.

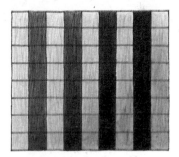

▲The strips should be taped together at the back and then ruled into squares for cutting.

▲Move every alternate strip one square along and trim off the extra squares.

▲Glue the veneer mat firmly on to the baseboard. When dry, tidy up the edges.

Making the board

Accurate measurement is very important. Carefully cut **five** light-coloured strips of veneer, and **four** dark strips, each 40cm × 5cm.

Lay these strips face down in alternate colours. **Tape** the strips together – masking tape or sellotape can be used. **Sandpaper** the edges of the strips so they are level.

Turn this mat of strips **face up,** and with rule and set square mark off eight strips, as shown

above. Carefully **cut** along these pencil lines with your trimming knife and rule.

Now **move** every other horizontal strip one square to the left. **Tape** these together, on the top surface.

With the knife and rule, **cut off** the protruding white squares. **Remove** the tape from the back.

Glue the veneer mat to the baseboard, remove the top tape – and get your chessmen ready to play!

Answers to the quiz

Q–Q8 mate!
Black loses to a smothered mate. His King is trapped behind his own Pawns. And no black piece can capture the white Queen, or move between the Queen and King to block the check.

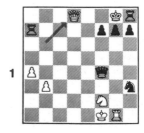

Q–B7 mate!
With this long move the white King is checked with no escape. The King can't take the black Queen because the Knight defends it. No other white piece can take the Queen either.

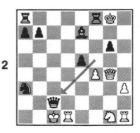

R–R8 mate!
The Rook moves the full length of the File, to combine with the other Rook to trap White in checkmate.

Always look for the quickest win. If the Queen had been taken instead, it would need many moves for Black to win.

Q–B7 wins!
Black King is forced to retreat into the corner so White then plays QxR ch. Black can bring his Bishop back to his B1 square to interpose but White then wins with QxB mate!

5   6   7

5.
B–Q7!
This is a 'discovered check'.
The Bishop moves, clearing the
File so that the Queen checks.
Black delays mate by one move,
with Q–B6. White plays QxQ
mate.

6.
PxN
This is the correct move. If you
play Bishop takes Queen, White
plays BxP, your King must move
K–K2 and White mates with
N–Q5! So the Knight must be
removed.

7.
PxN = N, mate!
The Pawn takes the Knight and
promotes into a Knight.
Normally Pawns promote into
Queens, but here it's quicker to
choose to become a Knight,
since that is checkmate.

8.
B–N7 mate!
The Knights are covering all the
possible escape squares. The
Bishop comes in to checkmate.
The King can't take the Bishop
because it's guarded by a
Knight.

9.
Q–R5 mate!
And the whole game lasted only
three moves! This shows how
easy it is to lose if you're
careless.

10.
QxBP mate!
Keep your own Pawn advances
to the centre, and hope for an
opponent like this!

11.
The board is the wrong way
round! The clocks should be in
one unit.

8   9   10

Reference section

Glossary

Board: there are 64 squares on a chess board, 32 white and 32 black. You should always check your right-hand corner square is white before playing.

Capture: chess pieces capture by occupying the square of an opponent's piece, which is then taken off the board.

Castling: a special move each player may make once in any game. It is the only time a player moves two of his own pieces in one move. The rules governing castling are on pages 22-23.

Check: the King is checked when a piece threatens to take it. The King must get out of check immediately.

Checkmate: when a King cannot escape from check, it is checkmate and the game is lost.

Development: to move Pawns forward or bring pieces out from the back Rank at the start of the game is to develop them.

Diagonals: the rows of squares, all the same colour, which run through the corners of the squares across the board.

Draw: when neither player can checkmate, the game is drawn.

End game: the final moves, when each player is trying to complete his plans to checkmate.

En passant: a special way for taking Pawns. See pages 24–25.

Exchange: when each player takes an enemy piece, it is called an exchange. You lose the exchange when the value of the piece you take is less than the value of the piece you lose.

File: one of the eight rows of squares, between a player and his opponent. These are the vertical rows in diagrams.

Fork: when a piece is able to take more than one enemy piece.

Gambit: the deliberate sacrifice of a piece (usually a Pawn), for positional advantage. The game on pages 38–39 starts with a gambit by White.

King's side: the right hand of the board for White, the left for Black. That is, the side of the board on which the King stands at the start.

Mate: checkmate.

Middle game: once the pieces are developed, the middle game begins.

Opening: the early moves, when each player moves his pieces into active positions.

Pawns: Each player has 8 Pawns. Any Pawn reaching the eighth Rank can be promoted.

Pieces: all the pieces are on the back Rank at the start of a game – two Rooks, two Knights, two Bishops, a King and a Queen for each player. Pawns are not usually called pieces.

Promotion: all Pawns can promote – no other piece. If a Pawn can advance to the eighth Rank without being taken, it becomes any piece the player decides on. This is usually a Queen.

Queen's side: the other side of the board from King's side – the left-hand side of the board for White and the right for Black.

Rank: the rows of squares which run from left to right across the board.

Sacrifice: allowing a piece to be taken to gain a better position.

Skewer: attacking a piece which shields a second opposing piece, with the aim of capturing the second.

Stalemate: if it is a player's turn to move, and there is no legal move he can make, that is stalemate, and a draw. Remember that a King is not allowed to move into check.

Swop: allowing one of your pieces to be taken, knowing you will recapture an opposing piece of equal value.

Threat: when a piece is on a square from which it can capture an opponent's piece.

Who starts?: White always starts and who plays White is decided by lottery. One player holds out a Pawn of each colour in his clenched fists. The opponent chooses, and plays the colour of the Pawn he selects.

How to find out more

MAGAZINES

British Chess Magazine
9 Market Street,
St Leonards on Sea,
East Sussex TN38 0DQ.

Chess
Sutton Coldfield, B73 6AZ.

BOOKS

History
A History of Chess, *by H. Golombek (Routledge & Kegan Paul)*

Tests
Chess – your move, *by Paul Langfield (Dent)*

Openings
Guide to Chess Openings, *by Leonard Barden and Tim Harding (Batsford)*

Chess Pieces
Chessmen, *by A. E. J. Mackett-Beeson (Weidenfeld & Nicolson)*

Improving play
Better Chess, *by Fred Reinfeld (Kaye & Ward)*

Champion games
Great Brilliancy Prize Games of the Chess Masters, *by Fred Reinfeld (Collier Macmillan)*

General
A Book of Chess, *by C. H. O'D. Alexander (Hutchinson)*

SUPPLIERS

Chess Centre,
3 Harcourt Street,
London W1

The Games Centre,
16 Hanway Street,
London W1A 2LS.
A wide catalogue of chess items, including Chinese and Japanese chess, and chess computers.

Supercast Limited,
Blanket Row,
Hull HU1 1SQ.
and
Impact Enterprises,
White Horse Yard,
North Street, Ripon,
Yorkshire, HG4 2HX.
Both of these companies can give full information on making your own chess set.

CASSETTES

Audio Chess,
7 Billockby Close,
Chessington,
Surrey KT9 2ED.
Recorded cassettes to help players improve their game.

Index